MW01206473

The Epic Summer Planner for Teens

Your Personal Guide to Your Best Summer Ever

For Cole and Patrick,
and all Epic Summer Adventurers

Table of Contents

Introduction

Welcome to your Best Summer Ever!

This summer you'll have over 1500 waking hours to work, play, and fight with your family.

But somehow summer can fly by and be over before you know it. Don't just find yourself three months from now sitting in a classroom again sporting new shoes and slightly darker tan, with a sense of déjà vu, wondering what happened to your summer.

Your mission this summer is to make a summer that goes down in your own personal history book, a truly great summer, The Best Summer Ever.

Figuring out what you really want to do at the beginning and doing it before summer is over is the key to having an Epic Summer.

Summer is your time to reclaim your dominion over yourself. The pages that follow are prompts to crafting your own personal vision of The Best Summer Ever. In Part 1 you'll take stock of your goals and interests, as well as think through the activities that you want to devote your time to this summer. You can use all that information to make sure that you spend your time doing the things that are really most meaningful to you, by using the daily planner pages in Part 2. If you ever find yourself shipwrecked in a sea of boredom or just looking for something new and different to spice up your summer, flip to Part 3 for a completely eclectic list of activities.

In Part 4, to be completed at the end of Summer, you'll take a look back and see how far you have come and all of the cool things you've done to create your truly Epic Summer!

Stop! Do Not Proceed to Summer.
Decompress.

Woo hoo! You're finally free! School's out! That alone should guarantee an Epic Summer, right?

Maybe not quite... Think of yourself as a rescued wild animal being returned to its natural habitat. You can't just jump back into the wild without being sure that you have the skills and are truly ready to really thrive out there this Summer.

Face it, you just spent the last 9 months in school, possibly the mental equivalent of ancient Japanese foot-binding. Your body has been in a chair far too long, and your relationships have been confined to the tiny screens on your electronic devices. You need REHABILITATION before you re-enter the wild.

What does your rehab that look like?

Do nothing! For a week. Veg out. Play video games. Binge watch whatever. Eat breakfast all day long. And definitely, wear pajamas all day, too.

It will drive your parents crazy, which is a perk. And after a while it will drive you crazy too, which is why you should only do this for a week and also why you will love your Epic Summer Planner, the blueprint for creating your Best Summer Ever.

So take one week off to completely decompress. And sometime during that first week, as your brain starts to clear and your imagination re-ignites, grab this book and begin architecting your Epic Summer.

You might be lucky and have the best ever summer by accident, but don't leave it to luck. Take a few minutes of planning to make sure that you have and Epic Summer!

Part 1: Taking Stock

Before you launch straight into summer, take some time to think about what is important to you this summer. The following pages are designed to help you think about what you WANT to do this summer, as well as to help you capture some of the things you need to do. Getting a handle on what's most important will give you a real head start to making this summer truly awesome. Just inviting and listening to your own thoughts is guaranteed to inspire and energize you. And capturing them here will help you develop the momentum you need to make it happen!

Life Dreams

Take a few moments to capture your dreams.

Imagine the best possible version of yourself... That might be tomorrow, in a year, in five or twenty...

Who do you want to be? What do you hope to achieve?

Your dreams are a fantastic guide to your unique destiny. Take a moment to get in touch with them, to allow them to ignite your imagination.

Paint a mental picture of your dreams, and draw or write them down here. Even if they change over time, these are your guides for now, and they'll be a fun time capsule to look back on!

Summer Goals

Don't settle for your life dreams being just dreams. Bring your visions closer to reality by thinking about what you might be able to do right now, this summer, to begin to build them for real!

There are lots of things you can do to begin to build the foundations for your dreams coming true right now, this summer.

If you dream of becoming an actor, perhaps you start by taking an acting class or auditioning for local summer productions. Or if you want to be a rock star, you can commit to practicing your guitar for 20 minutes every day. If you want to become an entrepreneur, you might start your own business right now – whether that is cleaning pools or dog-walking in your neighborhood. Or if you're not ready to start something, you can visit an entrepreneurial meetup to hear business plan pitches and startup war stories, or set aside time to read up on entrepreneurial best practices.

You get the idea. Think about your dreams, and then think of what things you might be able to do right now, with your free time this summer, to work towards your dream.

Next, spend thinking about other goals for this summer. These might not be dreams, but they are things you'd like to accomplish for yourself. They might be building towards a future goal or just fun goals in their own right. Write those down too!

If you want to buy a car next year, you might set a goal to save $1,000 from a summer job. You might want to play in tennis tournaments to earn a USTA rating. Or you might want to become a better swimmer. Or earn a merit badge towards Eagle Scout. Or lose 10 pounds. Or find a new friend group. Or learn French.

You get the idea. Think of some cool self-improvement projects you can do with the gift of time this summer. Write them down.

My Goals

Bad Habits? New Habits?

Have you noticed anything about yourself this past year that you'd like to change? Whether it's nail-biting or swearing, shoplifting or vaping, no bad habit is to small or too large to consider dropping.

This isn't about judgement and being perfect. The bottom line is, if there is something that you regularly do, that you wish you didn't do and can't seem to stop doing, or something that you know really bothers people around you frequently, that might be a bad habit. If it bothers you or creates problems for you, now is definitely a good time to quit. Habits generally only get worse on their own.

Summer is the perfect time to drop a habit that you want to get rid of, because you're out of the old routine, with all of the usual habit triggers. You have the advantage of restructuring your time and activities to avoid things that might trigger your habits and do things that promote good habits you would like to develop.

And, if you don't think you have any bad habits, just ask your family. ☺

On the flip side, you may have ideas on new good habits you want to develop. Whether it's simply flossing each morning or starting a daily workout or meditation practice, you can take advantage of your new summer schedule to carve out the time and experiment with making new habits work in your day.

They say it only takes 21 days to make a new habit. Whether that is exactly true or not isn't important. You have 100 days to start working towards the habits that you think will improve your life. Go for it!

Habit Hit List

Old Bad Habits	Game Plan for Change

New Good Habits	Game Plan For Change

New Skills

Is there something you have always been interested in but haven't had a chance to try, or maybe you've tried it but haven't mastered it yet? Kayaking, drawing manga, sewing, rock climbing, film making, yodeling...?

Or is there a skill that you think might be important for your future success that you want to begin to develop? Public speaking, personal finance, HTML coding?

Make it a goal to find opportunities to explore your budding interests this summer! You have the time now. A quick internet search will reveal lots of ways, from YouTube videos to local courses, that you can begin to explore your interests. And don't forget to use your social networks to find people who would be happy to help you in your quest.

Skills I Want to Develop & Resources

Save Up

If you've got a summer job, you're about to start raking in the cash. But it's amazing how quickly that hard-earned cash can vanish if you don't have a solid plan for saving, especially during summer. Each little latte and lemonade all add up in the end.

The surest way to make sure that you have savings at the end of the summer is to always deduct your savings from you pay check, right away, right off of the top. Transfer your savings to a different account if you need to, and keep them safe and "off limits" from spending, no matter what.

You may have a specific goal you are saving for, like saving towards college or saving for a car. Or you may just want to end the summer with a certain amount in the bank to last you through the next school year. No matter what, take some time to figure out how much money you need to save, and then make a budget around that. And stick to it! This is your hard earned money!

My savings goal $_____

My expected earnings $_____

My disposable income $_____

My weekly spending budget $_____

Be Curious

What would you like to learn more about? Take a minute to think of things that might piqued your interest during school but which you didn't have time to explore as you were force-fed seven subjects for eight hours a day.

It could be something that you touched on briefly in school, but didn't have time to really explore, like Egyptian gods, how hurricanes form, combustion engines, or what was it like to be Vincent Van Gogh? You can take some time now to explore those things. Get on the internet, or go to your cool airconditioned library to pick up a great biography or how-to manual.

Or maybe there's something that you were daydreaming about in school while you were locked up in the classroom – maybe it's doing something with your hands like learning to throw pottery on a wheel or starting a vegetable garden.

This is also the perfect chance to do a little research on your dreams and goals. Find out what it really takes to train and qualify for the Tour de France or an Everest ascent. The point is, you have all summer now to focus on what is interesting to YOU. Sure, you will want to binge watch some Netflix and play Fortnight, but don't fall into a summer-slob rut. Set a timer for your electronics, clear your brain, and make some space to explore new frontiers.

Pick some wild hair ideas that you might like to explore. Do a little research and follow the trail as long as it interests you, and when you're satisfied, stop. There's no research paper due!

Last of all, this is a totally retro idea, but seriously try it: Go to your library. It's cool and quiet on a hot day. Idly browse through the stacks and see what looks interesting. Check out a stack of books – whatever strikes your fancy. Cookbooks, Car & Driver magazines, romance novels, travel guides, how-to knit, whatever!

Curiosities

Read

"What? Read on my summer break? No way!"

You might think that this is a bait and switch for a program that promises the Best Summer Ever, but reading is truly a part of having an Epic Summer.

This summer, pick a few titles to read purely for ENJOYMENT. Even if they are comic books, that's OK, but trust me young Padawan, you will soon realize the power of reading over the summer. And at the very least, if the words "There's nothing to do" ever escape your lips, you can solve that problem by diving into a good book for a while.

So take a minute, right now, to list a few books or topics that you want to read about over the summer. Pick them up from the library as you go, and always have one or two on hand. Then chip away every day or devour them in a weekend. Set yourself a goal of reading until it feels fun again!

My Summer Book List

Plan a trip

One of the time-honored highlights of summer is the "Family Summer Vacation". Whether you love them or dread them because your family travels like the Griswolds, now is the perfect time for you to start taking a bigger role in planning the trip that you would like to have.

Your family might not have the means to do the trip of your dreams, but regardless of what your situation and budget are, you can become a chief architect.

Planning a trip is a great way to develop a lot of the executive skills that you will use through your whole life – establishing a budget, researching viable options, creating an itinerary and a schedule, charting the route, making reservations, and so on.

Your anticipation will grow as you put the trip together, right down to what rest stops you'll hit and whether to detour off of the interstate to see the world's largest ball of twine. Plus, it's so much more fun to arrive in a place having already researched what you want to do there.

Work with your parents right up front, and let them know that you're signed up to be a key contributor to the planning process. Then unleash your inner adventurer on the internet to learn all you can about your destination and the logistics of making it happen.

And if a big family vacation is not in the cards for you this year, you still can plan a trip! A weekend at a state park campground 90 minutes from home won't set you back much and still will use all of your great imagination and planning skills. Or draw a circle in a three to five hour radius from home and do a weekend road trip. Even a stay-cation works. It's a rite of summer. Plan that trip!

Move it!

Your body has been molded into right angles for the last nine months sitting in plastic chairs for hours on end, and now is the time to rehabilitate it!

Stretch it, swing it, shake it – get it moving again so you're not cursed with the posture of a boiled shrimp by the time you graduate.

It doesn't matter what you do – just do it! The best exercise is the one that you will do. Swimming, running, climbing, yoga, weights... whatever you enjoy most is what you should do.

And consider working out with a friend to maximize the fun and also to keep yourselves accountable to your workout routine.

Of course you can definitely mix it up. You might run or lift with a friend three days a week but then play sand volleyball or swim on the other days.

You can also take the opportunity to try new things over the summer. Badminton, anyone?

And don't forget in a pinch, good old walking is great exercise and totally underrated. Just put your shoes on and get out the door.

The most important tip here is to carve out the time, every day, when you will work out or do whatever kind of physical activity you come up with. Make a date with yourself (or with your friends), and stick to it. Your body will LOVE you for it.

MY PHYSICAL PLAN

Make a difference

Ah Summer! Time indulge yourself! That is totally the best part of summer, for sure. That's what we all did back when we were little kids, partly because we couldn't really do anything else.

But now that you're older and more capable, it's a great opportunity to spread your wings and use your summer to lift up the world around you.

Think of a cause or an organization that really speaks to your values and interests. See what you can do to help, and budget some time to get involved. It could be anything from working in a community garden to walking the dogs at the Humane Society, tutoring young kids who struggle with reading, or visiting a senior center to play cards with the residents.

Spreading a little bit of YOU around makes the world a much better place. And you'll be amazed about how good you will feel about yourself. Doing good for others is one of the best ways to feel better about yourself. It's magic.

Even if you can't volunteer your time because of other commitments, you can take the time to get informed about the issues and needs in your community or on our planet.

Use the following worksheet to think through and gather information on the issues and organizations that can provide meaningful opportunities to make a difference. What grabs your heart?

Which issues do I care about?

Which organizations focus on my issue?

What kind of help is needed?

What specifically can I do?

Overachieve

OK, some people are overachievers. You know who you are. And you are awesome! You probably already have some ideas of how to get a jump on the coming school year, so feel free to skip ahead.

If you're not a natural born overachiever, and are wondering why anyone would want to be, then let me just ask this:

If by doing a little bit of prep work this summer at your leisure, you could make your life a lot easier and freer during the school year, would you want to?

Previewing the material for next year is an excellent way to rock it when you tackle it for real in school. All of the latest science on studying and memory show that repetition is the key. So if you sometimes find classroom lectures boring and unmemorable, and that gets in the way of getting the grades you want, you might consider previewing the material over the summer. That way, when your geometry teacher gives a 3 minute overview of how to calculate the volume of a cylinder, you won't be scribbling notes for dear life. Instead you'll be thinking "Oh, yeah, I remember that. That makes sense." as you write a few refresher notes. You'll be in the driver's seat, recognizing and reinforcing ideas that you've already seen before, rather than scrambling to keep up.

And previewing doesn't have to be painful. I'm not talking about reading the whole Chemistry text book ahead of time, although you might want want to order your book early and skim the first ten chapters for highlights. And there are lots of ways to prepare for material if you don't have the book yet. For example, you can learn the periodic table or watch Kahn Academy or other videos to preview the information.

Or just watch your favorite re-runs in Spanish. It all adds up!

Overachiever Goals

Course	Target

Get Out!

This is what we did during summer back in the 1900's... we went outside, pretty much all summer long. Yes, we had TV (in color) and air conditioning, and even Atari, and we enjoyed them. But back in the day, most of summer was spent, and certainly the best memories were made, OUTSIDE.

You don't have to suffer like a contestant on Survivor, but get yourself outside, at least once a day. And not just from the parking lot to the mall, that doesn't count. Take your shoes off and feel the grass. Take a walk. Swim. Play tag with some little kids or touch football with your friends. Catch fireflies again.

Those nine months spent in school can be a little too civilizing sometimes. Your inner wild thing is crying out to get outside.

I know, that first blast of hot air as you emerge from the A/C makes you want to dash back inside like a turtle into its shell, but take your time, move slowly, and acclimate to the great outdoors. It's totally worth it.

When you get outside, you open up another dimension of yourself that has been locked away in a school building too long. This isn't just about getting your body moving, it's about your mental health too. Sitting in your PJ's playing video games or binge watching Netflix all day is like the mental equivalent of eating nothing but donuts. It's just unhealthy. A shot of sunshine, or even rain, will do wonders for your mental health. In fact, whenever you find yourself getting down or feeling blue this summer, do this: Put your shoes on, and get out the door. Try to go for a walk, but if all you do is to just put your shoes on, get out the door, and stand on the porch, you will find that it does wonders for your mood. Bonus, you can do this all year long too!

Pull Your Weight

We saved the not-best for last. Chores. Sadly, they are undeniable and unavoidable. But they are much more manageable and much less burdensome with a little organization. And let's face it, the two hours spent procrastinating and avoiding a twenty minute chore is just two hours wasted in a state of low energy angst. The best strategy is to plan the chore, skip the fretting and agonizing, and just get it done. Structure is your friend. Plan your chores, knock them out, and get back to having fun on your own agenda.

If you're like most people, your parents are probably financing most of your summer fun. And the labor value of your chores probably doesn't cover the bill. So try to make your contribution cheerfully.

Take a minute to list out your basic summer chores and when you'll do them. Bonus points for making a plan to do them without being reminded!

Regular chores:

Ideas for bonus chores to delight your folks:

Part 2 - Bring it All Together

You have looked at your dreams and goals, stoked your imagination, committed to developing your mind and body, and even thought about how to make the world a better place.

What you have written in the preceding pages is inspired stuff! It's the ingredient list for cooking up the Best Summer Ever. But just like baking cookies, there's a little more to it than just gathering all of the ingredients together. Now it's time for a little processing.

So the question is: How are you going to make it happen?

The answer is…. Write it down, in your planner. Every day.

Nothing happens on it's own, and your blueprint to the Best Summer Ever won't help you unless you use it and put your ideas into action by planning out your days.

Ugh! That might sound like work, but actually what could be more fun than actively planning out doing all of the cool things that you've decided to do?

Each day, start your day by simply taking a couple of minutes to select your priorities from your amazing inspired lists of things to do, and give them a place in your day. That way you can both look forward to them and also make sure that they happen.

You are taking charge of your summer, and you will feel great about how much you accomplish with a little planning. People who plan achieve.

So don't stop now. Take the reigns, and make it an Epic Summer!

Using the Planner

Your Epic Summer Planner has 100 daily planner pages, approximately one for each day between Memorial Day and Labor Day.

Start Your Day Right!

First thing each morning, start your day by filling out your daily Goals and To-Do's. This is where you bring all of your ideas from the preceding pages to life. Take your goals and fun ideas, and break them into daily bite-sized chunks. Jot down a few for today, and presto, you have your action plan for the day. If you don't have any ideas off the top of your head, just browse back through your planner and choose a few that strike your fancy. Or if you're in a funk, browse the "Help, I'm bored!" section and find some off-the wall activity to shake things up from your normal routine. Go ahead and circle the box next to anything on your list that is really important or exciting. Focus on those as your priority for the day.

While you're planning your main activities today, also make a plan to do one "act of kindness" for someone sometime today. It doesn't have to be big, but come up with a specific idea right now and write it down. That's the best guarantee that it will happen.

Next, make a note of any calendar commitments or appointments you have, like work, a team practice, or getting together with a friend.

As you go through your day, check the box or cross off the items on your list as you accomplish them. Don't skip this – it feels good to knock down your lists! Since it's summer, you don't have to finish every item on your list each day, of course. Feel free to roll them into tomorrow. But do keep track of them!

Now, do one of the most important things on the page. Write down something **GOOD** about yourself. And do yourself justice! Take a moment to think of something new and different each day. You will not run out of material, but at first you might feel stuck because you're not used to admitting how great you are. Hang with this until you find some fresh new thing each day that is smile-worthy about you. It can be as simple as your great laugh, or as impressive as your ability to speak three languages fluently. Admit your greatness each day this summer. If something doesn't come to you at the start of the day, you can do it later during the day or at the end of the day. But do not ever skip this step!

Finally, either first thing or at some point during your day, take time to list three things you are grateful for. These don't have to be complicated, but again, be thoughtful and try to keep it interesting and non-repetitive. Just taking a moment to recognize gratitude for the good things in your life, whether it's a special friendship or a seeing a bluebird, is super important. Gratitude is scientifically proven to improve your physical and psychological health and your relationships, and it's free! Don't skip this step!

Random notes is just a space for you to capture anything that pops up during the day that you need to keep track of – or doodle!

At the End of the Day...

Simply making plans in the morning and writing them down vastly increases your chances of having all of that good stuff happen. Take a minute to review your list, crossing off any items, or adding new ideas for tomorrow. If you didn't already write down your great thing about yourself and your gratitudes, do that now, too.

Take a moment to relax and think back on everything that has happened today. What were the highlights? Write these down. Savor them.

Finally, capture reflections from your day in the Journal section. You have a unique perspective in this universe. Honor it here.

Start this day!

Today is: __June 1 Sample__

Goals & To Do's

- ☑ Run 2 miles
- ☐ Bake cookies
- ☑ Read 30 min
- ☐ Practice guitar
- ☑ Call Humane Society
- ☑ Spanish Duolingo
- ☑ Take out trash
- ☐
- ☐
- ☐

Pre-planned kindness:

Call grandma to say hi

Tic toc! Appointments
- ☺ Coffee with Maya @ 9
- ☺ Dentist @ 4
- ☺

Something great about me

My singing voice

3 Gratitudes

I got the job!
My dog loves me
Ice cream in the freezer

Random Notes

Call Steph back

Today's highlights...   Best thing that happened... I did good...
Something I learned... I'm going to dream about... The funniest...

The pool! Nate is totally insane. Seeing Katie do a duck walk.
I invited Suz to come with us ☺
Road trip to Michigan?

Journal

I got the job at the zoo! Totally psyched and scared too
Can't wait to make $ for new guitar! #almost famous
I totally didn't want to invite Suz to the pool, but it was huge
for her and it didn't hurt me. I'm glad I did.

Start this day!

Today is: _____

Goals & To Do's

☐

☐

☐

☐

☐

☐

☐

☐

☐

☐

Pre-planned kindness:

Tic toc! Appointments

🕐

🕐

🕐

Something great about me

3 Gratitudes

Random Notes

Today's highlights... Best thing that happened... I did good...
Something I learned... I'm going to dream about... The funniest...

Journal

_____

_____

_____

_____

Start this day!

Today is: _____

Goals & To Do's

☐

☐

☐

☐

☐

☐

☐

☐

☐

☐

Pre-planned kindness:

Tic toc! Appointments

🕐

🕐

🕐

Something great about me

3 Gratitudes

Random Notes

Today's highlights... Best thing that happened... I did good...
Something I learned... I'm going to dream about... The funniest...

Journal

_____

_____

_____

_____

Start this day!

Today is: _____

Goals & To Do's

- ☐
- ☐
- ☐
- ☐
- ☐
- ☐
- ☐
- ☐
- ☐
- ☐

Pre-planned kindness:

Tic toc! Appointments

🕐
🕐
🕐

Something great about me

3 Gratitudes

Random Notes

Today's highlights... Best thing that happened... I did good...
Something I learned... I'm going to dream about... The funniest...

Journal

_____
_____
_____
_____

Start this day!

Today is: _____

Goals & To Do's

- [ ]
- [ ]
- [ ]
- [ ]
- [ ]
- [ ]
- [ ]
- [ ]
- [ ]
- [ ]

Pre-planned kindness:

Tic toc! Appointments

- 🕐
- 🕐
- 🕐

Something great about me

3 Gratitudes

Random Notes

Today's highlights... Best thing that happened... I did good...
Something I learned... I'm going to dream about... The funniest...

Journal

_____

_____

_____

_____

Start this day!

Today is: _____

Goals & To Do's

☐

☐

☐

☐

☐

☐

☐

☐

☐

☐

Pre-planned kindness:

Tic toc! Appointments

🕐

🕐

🕐

Something great about me

3 Gratitudes

Random Notes

Today's highlights... Best thing that happened... I did good...
Something I learned... I'm going to dream about... The funniest...

Journal

_____

_____

_____

_____

Start this day!

Today is: _____

Goals & To Do's

☐

☐

☐

☐

☐

☐

☐

☐

☐

☐

Pre-planned kindness:

Tic toc! Appointments

🕐

🕐

🕐

Something great about me

3 Gratitudes

Random Notes

Today's highlights... Best thing that happened... I did good...
Something I learned... I'm going to dream about... The funniest...

Journal

_____

_____

_____

_____

Start this day!

Today is: _____

Goals & To Do's

☐
☐
☐
☐
☐
☐
☐
☐
☐
☐

Pre-planned kindness:

Tic toc! Appointments

🕐
🕐
🕐

Something great about me

3 Gratitudes

Random Notes

Today's highlights... Best thing that happened... I did good...
Something I learned... I'm going to dream about... The funniest...

Journal

_____
_____
_____
_____

Start this day!

Today is: _____

Goals & To Do's

- ☐
- ☐
- ☐
- ☐
- ☐
- ☐
- ☐
- ☐
- ☐
- ☐

Pre-planned kindness:

Tic toc! Appointments

🕐
🕐
🕐

Something great about me

3 Gratitudes

Random Notes

Today's highlights... Best thing that happened... I did good...
Something I learned... I'm going to dream about... The funniest...

Journal

_____
_____
_____
_____

Start this day!

Today is: _____

Goals & To Do's

☐

☐

☐

☐

☐

☐

☐

☐

☐

☐

Pre-planned kindness:

Tic toc! Appointments

🕐

🕐

🕐

Something great about me

3 Gratitudes

Random Notes

Today's highlights... Best thing that happened... I did good...
Something I learned... I'm going to dream about... The funniest...

Journal

_____

_____

_____

_____

Start this day!

Today is: _____

Goals & To Do's

- ☐
- ☐
- ☐
- ☐
- ☐
- ☐
- ☐
- ☐
- ☐
- ☐

Pre-planned kindness:

Tic toc! Appointments

🕐
🕐
🕐

Something great about me

3 Gratitudes

Random Notes

Today's highlights... Best thing that happened... I did good...
Something I learned... I'm going to dream about... The funniest...

Journal

_____
_____
_____
_____

Start this day!

Today is: _____

Goals & To Do's

☐
☐
☐
☐
☐
☐
☐
☐
☐
☐

Pre-planned kindness:

Tic toc! Appointments

🕐
🕐
🕐

Something great about me

3 Gratitudes

Random Notes

Today's highlights... Best thing that happened... I did good...
Something I learned... I'm going to dream about... The funniest...

Journal

_____
_____
_____
_____

Start this day!

Today is: _____

Goals & To Do's

- ☐
- ☐
- ☐
- ☐
- ☐
- ☐
- ☐
- ☐
- ☐
- ☐

Pre-planned kindness:

Tic toc! Appointments

- 🕐
- 🕐
- 🕐

Something great about me

3 Gratitudes

Random Notes

Today's highlights... Best thing that happened... I did good...
Something I learned... I'm going to dream about... The funniest...

Journal

_____
_____
_____
_____

Start this day!

Today is: _____

Goals & To Do's

- ☐
- ☐
- ☐
- ☐
- ☐
- ☐
- ☐
- ☐
- ☐
- ☐

Pre-planned kindness:

Tic toc! Appointments

- ⊘
- ⊘
- ⊘

Something great about me

3 Gratitudes

Random Notes

Today's highlights... Best thing that happened... I did good...
Something I learned... I'm going to dream about... The funniest...

Journal

_____

_____

_____

_____

Start this day!

Today is: _____

Goals & To Do's

☐
☐
☐
☐
☐
☐
☐
☐
☐
☐

Pre-planned kindness:

Tic toc! Appointments

🕐
🕐
🕐

Something great about me

3 Gratitudes

Random Notes

Today's highlights... Best thing that happened... I did good...
Something I learned... I'm going to dream about... The funniest...

Journal

_____
_____
_____
_____

Start this day!

Today is: _____

Goals & To Do's

☐
☐
☐
☐
☐
☐
☐
☐
☐
☐

Pre-planned kindness:

Tic toc! Appointments

🕐
🕐
🕐

Something great about me

3 Gratitudes

Random Notes

Today's highlights... Best thing that happened... I did good...
Something I learned... I'm going to dream about... The funniest...

Journal

_____
_____
_____
_____

Start this day!

Today is: _____

Goals & To Do's

☐
☐
☐
☐
☐
☐
☐
☐
☐
☐

Pre-planned kindness:

Tic toc! Appointments

🕐
🕐
🕐

Something great about me

3 Gratitudes

Random Notes

Today's highlights... Best thing that happened... I did good...
Something I learned... I'm going to dream about... The funniest...

Journal

_____
_____
_____
_____

Start this day!

Today is: _____

Goals & To Do's

- ☐
- ☐
- ☐
- ☐
- ☐
- ☐
- ☐
- ☐
- ☐
- ☐

Pre-planned kindness:

Tic toc! Appointments

- ⏱
- ⏱
- ⏱

Something great about me

3 Gratitudes

Random Notes

Today's highlights... Best thing that happened... I did good...
Something I learned... I'm going to dream about... The funniest...

Journal

_____
_____
_____
_____

Start this day!

Today is: _____

Goals & To Do's

☐
☐
☐
☐
☐
☐
☐
☐
☐
☐

Pre-planned kindness:

Tic toc! Appointments

🕐
🕐
🕐

Something great about me

3 Gratitudes

Random Notes

Today's highlights... Best thing that happened... I did good...
Something I learned... I'm going to dream about... The funniest...

Journal

_____
_____
_____
_____

Start this day!

Today is: _____

Goals & To Do's

- ☐
- ☐
- ☐
- ☐
- ☐
- ☐
- ☐
- ☐
- ☐
- ☐

Pre-planned kindness:

Tic toc! Appointments

🕐
🕐
🕐

Something great about me

3 Gratitudes

Random Notes

Today's highlights... Best thing that happened... I did good...
Something I learned... I'm going to dream about... The funniest...

Journal

_____

_____

_____

_____

Start this day!

Today is: _____

Goals & To Do's

- ☐
- ☐
- ☐
- ☐
- ☐
- ☐
- ☐
- ☐
- ☐
- ☐

Pre-planned kindness:

Tic toc! Appointments

🕐
🕐
🕐

Something great about me

3 Gratitudes

Random Notes

Today's highlights... Best thing that happened... I did good...
Something I learned... I'm going to dream about... The funniest...

Journal

_____

_____

_____

_____

Start this day!

Today is: _____

Goals & To Do's

- ☐
- ☐
- ☐
- ☐
- ☐
- ☐
- ☐
- ☐
- ☐
- ☐

Pre-planned kindness:

Tic toc! Appointments

- ☉
- ☉
- ☉

Something great about me

3 Gratitudes

Random Notes

Today's highlights... Best thing that happened... I did good...
Something I learned... I'm going to dream about... The funniest...

Journal

_____
_____
_____
_____

Start this day!

Today is: _____

Goals & To Do's

☐

☐

☐

☐

☐

☐

☐

☐

☐

☐

Pre-planned kindness:

Tic toc! Appointments

🕐

🕐

🕐

Something great about me

3 Gratitudes

Random Notes

Today's highlights... Best thing that happened... I did good...
Something I learned... I'm going to dream about... The funniest...

Journal

_____

_____

_____

_____

Start this day!

Today is: _____

Goals & To Do's

- ☐
- ☐
- ☐
- ☐
- ☐
- ☐
- ☐
- ☐
- ☐
- ☐

Pre-planned kindness:

Tic toc! Appointments

🕐
🕐
🕐

Something great about me

3 Gratitudes

Random Notes

Today's highlights... Best thing that happened... I did good...
Something I learned... I'm going to dream about... The funniest...

Journal

_____
_____
_____
_____

Start this day!

Today is:_____

Goals & To Do's

☐

☐

☐

☐

☐

☐

☐

☐

☐

☐

Pre-planned kindness:

Tic toc! Appointments

🕐

🕐

🕐

Something great about me

3 Gratitudes

Random Notes

Today's highlights... Best thing that happened... I did good...
Something I learned... I'm going to dream about... The funniest...

Journal

_____

_____

_____

_____

Start this day!

Today is: _____

Goals & To Do's

- ☐
- ☐
- ☐
- ☐
- ☐
- ☐
- ☐
- ☐
- ☐
- ☐

Pre-planned kindness:

Tic toc! Appointments

🕐
🕐
🕐

Something great about me

3 Gratitudes

Random Notes

Today's highlights... Best thing that happened... I did good...
Something I learned... I'm going to dream about... The funniest...

Journal

_____
_____
_____
_____

Start this day!

Today is: _____

Goals & To Do's

- ☐
- ☐
- ☐
- ☐
- ☐
- ☐
- ☐
- ☐
- ☐
- ☐

Pre-planned kindness:

Tic toc! Appointments

- ⏲
- ⏲
- ⏲

Something great about me

3 Gratitudes

Random Notes

Today's highlights... Best thing that happened... I did good...
Something I learned... I'm going to dream about... The funniest...

Journal

_____

_____

_____

_____

Start this day!

Today is: _____

Goals & To Do's

☐

☐

☐

☐

☐

☐

☐

☐

☐

☐

Pre-planned kindness:

Tic toc! Appointments

⏱

⏱

⏱

Something great about me

3 Gratitudes

Random Notes

Today's highlights... Best thing that happened... I did good...
Something I learned... I'm going to dream about... The funniest...

Journal

_____

_____

_____

_____

Start this day!

Today is: _____

Goals & To Do's

☐

☐

☐

☐

☐

☐

☐

☐

☐

☐

Pre-planned kindness:

Tic toc! Appointments

🕐

🕐

🕐

Something great about me

3 Gratitudes

Random Notes

Today's highlights... Best thing that happened... I did good...
Something I learned... I'm going to dream about... The funniest...

Journal

_____

_____

_____

_____

Start this day!

Today is: _____

Goals & To Do's

- ☐
- ☐
- ☐
- ☐
- ☐
- ☐
- ☐
- ☐
- ☐
- ☐

Pre-planned kindness:

Tic toc! Appointments

- 🕐
- 🕐
- 🕐

Something great about me

3 Gratitudes

Random Notes

Today's highlights... Best thing that happened... I did good...
Something I learned... I'm going to dream about... The funniest...

Journal

_____
_____
_____
_____

Start this day!

Today is: _____

Goals & To Do's

- [ ]
- [ ]
- [ ]
- [ ]
- [ ]
- [ ]
- [ ]
- [ ]
- [ ]
- [ ]

Pre-planned kindness:

Tic toc! Appointments

- 🕐
- 🕐
- 🕐

Something great about me

3 Gratitudes

Random Notes

Today's highlights... Best thing that happened... I did good...
Something I learned... I'm going to dream about... The funniest...

Journal

_____

_____

_____

_____

Start this day!

Today is: _____

Goals & To Do's

☐
☐
☐
☐
☐
☐
☐
☐
☐
☐

Pre-planned kindness:

Tic toc! Appointments

🕐
🕐
🕐

Something great about me

3 Gratitudes

Random Notes

Today's highlights... Best thing that happened... I did good...
Something I learned... I'm going to dream about... The funniest...

Journal

_____

_____

_____

_____

Start this day!

Today is: _____

Goals & To Do's

- ☐
- ☐
- ☐
- ☐
- ☐
- ☐
- ☐
- ☐
- ☐
- ☐

Pre-planned kindness:

Tic toc! Appointments

🕐
🕐
🕐

Something great about me

3 Gratitudes

Random Notes

Today's highlights... Best thing that happened... I did good...
Something I learned... I'm going to dream about... The funniest...

Journal

_____

_____

_____

_____

Start this day!

Today is: _____

Goals & To Do's

☐
☐
☐
☐
☐
☐
☐
☐
☐
☐

Pre-planned kindness:

Tic toc! Appointments

⊘
⊘
⊘

Something great about me

3 Gratitudes

Random Notes

Today's highlights... Best thing that happened... I did good...
Something I learned... I'm going to dream about... The funniest...

Journal

_____
_____
_____
_____

Start this day!

Today is: _____

Goals & To Do's

- ☐
- ☐
- ☐
- ☐
- ☐
- ☐
- ☐
- ☐
- ☐
- ☐

Pre-planned kindness:

Tic toc! Appointments

- 🕐
- 🕐
- 🕐

Something great about me

3 Gratitudes

Random Notes

Today's highlights... Best thing that happened... I did good... Something I learned... I'm going to dream about... The funniest...

Journal

_____

_____

_____

_____

Start this day!

Today is: _____

Goals & To Do's

☐

☐

☐

☐

☐

☐

☐

☐

☐

☐

Pre-planned kindness:

Tic toc! Appointments

🕐

🕐

🕐

Something great about me

3 Gratitudes

Random Notes

Today's highlights... Best thing that happened... I did good...
Something I learned... I'm going to dream about... The funniest...

Journal

_____

_____

_____

_____

Start this day!

Today is: _____

Goals & To Do's

☐

☐

☐

☐

☐

☐

☐

☐

☐

☐

Pre-planned kindness:

Tic toc! Appointments

🕐

🕐

🕐

Something great about me

3 Gratitudes

Random Notes

Today's highlights... Best thing that happened... I did good...
Something I learned... I'm going to dream about... The funniest...

Journal

_____

_____

_____

_____

Start this day!

Today is: _____

Goals & To Do's

- [ ]
- [ ]
- [ ]
- [ ]
- [ ]
- [ ]
- [ ]
- [ ]
- [ ]
- [ ]

Pre-planned kindness:

Tic toc! Appointments

- ⏱
- ⏱
- ⏱

Something great about me

3 Gratitudes

Random Notes

Today's highlights... Best thing that happened... I did good...
Something I learned... I'm going to dream about... The funniest...

Journal

_____
_____
_____
_____

Start this day!

Today is: _____

Goals & To Do's

- ☐
- ☐
- ☐
- ☐
- ☐
- ☐
- ☐
- ☐
- ☐
- ☐

Pre-planned kindness:

Tic toc! Appointments

🕐
🕐
🕐

Something great about me

3 Gratitudes

Random Notes

Today's highlights... Best thing that happened... I did good...
Something I learned... I'm going to dream about... The funniest...

Journal

_____

_____

_____

_____

Start this day!

Today is: _____

Goals & To Do's

- ☐
- ☐
- ☐
- ☐
- ☐
- ☐
- ☐
- ☐
- ☐
- ☐

Pre-planned kindness:

Tic toc! Appointments

🕐
🕐
🕐

Something great about me

3 Gratitudes

Random Notes

Today's highlights... Best thing that happened... I did good...
Something I learned... I'm going to dream about... The funniest...

Journal

_____

_____

_____

_____

Start this day!

Today is: _____

Goals & To Do's

- ☐
- ☐
- ☐
- ☐
- ☐
- ☐
- ☐
- ☐
- ☐
- ☐

Pre-planned kindness:

Tic toc! Appointments

- 🕐
- 🕐
- 🕐

Something great about me

3 Gratitudes

Random Notes

Today's highlights... Best thing that happened... I did good...
Something I learned... I'm going to dream about... The funniest...

Journal

_____

_____

_____

_____

Start this day!

Today is: _____

Goals & To Do's

☐

☐

☐

☐

☐

☐

☐

☐

☐

☐

Pre-planned kindness:

Tic toc! Appointments

🕐

🕐

🕐

Something great about me

3 Gratitudes

Random Notes

Today's highlights... Best thing that happened... I did good...
Something I learned... I'm going to dream about... The funniest...

Journal

_____

_____

_____

_____

Start this day!

Today is: _____

Goals & To Do's

- ☐
- ☐
- ☐
- ☐
- ☐
- ☐
- ☐
- ☐
- ☐
- ☐

Pre-planned kindness:

Tic toc! Appointments

- 🕐
- 🕐
- 🕐

Something great about me

3 Gratitudes

Random Notes

Today's highlights... Best thing that happened... I did good...
Something I learned... I'm going to dream about... The funniest...

Journal

_____

_____

_____

_____

Start this day!

Today is: _____

Goals & To Do's

☐
☐
☐
☐
☐
☐
☐
☐
☐
☐

Pre-planned kindness:

Tic toc! Appointments

🕐
🕐
🕐

Something great about me

3 Gratitudes

Random Notes

Today's highlights... Best thing that happened... I did good...
Something I learned... I'm going to dream about... The funniest...

Journal

_____
_____
_____
_____

Start this day!

Today is: _____

Goals & To Do's

- ☐
- ☐
- ☐
- ☐
- ☐
- ☐
- ☐
- ☐
- ☐
- ☐

Pre-planned kindness:

Tic toc! Appointments

🕐
🕐
🕐

Something great about me

3 Gratitudes

Random Notes

Today's highlights... Best thing that happened... I did good...
Something I learned... I'm going to dream about... The funniest...

Journal

_____
_____
_____
_____

Start this day!

Today is: _____

Goals & To Do's

☐

☐

☐

☐

☐

☐

☐

☐

☐

☐

Pre-planned kindness:

Tic toc! Appointments

🕐

🕐

🕐

Something great about me

3 Gratitudes

Random Notes

Today's highlights... Best thing that happened... I did good...
Something I learned... I'm going to dream about... The funniest...

Journal

_____

_____

_____

_____

Start this day!

Goals & To Do's

☐
☐
☐
☐
☐
☐
☐
☐
☐
☐

Pre-planned kindness:

Tic toc! Appointments

🕐
🕐
🕐

Something great about me

3 Gratitudes

Random Notes

Today's highlights... Best thing that happened... I did good...
Something I learned... I'm going to dream about... The funniest...

Journal

_____

_____

_____

_____

Start this day!

Today is: _____

Goals & To Do's

☐

☐

☐

☐

☐

☐

☐

☐

☐

☐

Pre-planned kindness:

Tic toc! Appointments

🕐

🕐

🕐

Something great about me

3 Gratitudes

Random Notes

Today's highlights... Best thing that happened... I did good...
Something I learned... I'm going to dream about... The funniest...

Journal

_____

_____

_____

_____

Start this day!

Today is: _____

Goals & To Do's

☐
☐
☐
☐
☐
☐
☐
☐
☐
☐

Pre-planned kindness:

Tic toc! Appointments

⊘
⊘
⊘

Something great about me

3 Gratitudes

Random Notes

Today's highlights... Best thing that happened... I did good...
Something I learned... I'm going to dream about... The funniest...

Journal

_____
_____
_____
_____

Start this day!

Today is: _____

Goals & To Do's

- [ ]
- [ ]
- [ ]
- [ ]
- [ ]
- [ ]
- [ ]
- [ ]
- [ ]
- [ ]

Pre-planned kindness:

Tic toc! Appointments

- 🕐
- 🕐
- 🕐

Something great about me

3 Gratitudes

Random Notes

Today's highlights... Best thing that happened... I did good...
Something I learned... I'm going to dream about... The funniest...

Journal

_____
_____
_____
_____

Start this day!

Today is: _____

Goals & To Do's

- ☐
- ☐
- ☐
- ☐
- ☐
- ☐
- ☐
- ☐
- ☐
- ☐

Pre-planned kindness:

Tic toc! Appointments

🕐
🕐
🕐

Something great about me

3 Gratitudes

Random Notes

Today's highlights... Best thing that happened... I did good...
Something I learned... I'm going to dream about... The funniest...

Journal

_____
_____
_____
_____

Start this day!

Today is: _____

Goals & To Do's

☐

☐

☐

☐

☐

☐

☐

☐

☐

☐

Pre-planned kindness:

Tic toc! Appointments

🕐

🕐

🕐

Something great about me

3 Gratitudes

Random Notes

Today's highlights... Best thing that happened... I did good...
Something I learned... I'm going to dream about... The funniest...

Journal

_____

_____

_____

_____

Start this day!

Today is: _____

Goals & To Do's

- ☐
- ☐
- ☐
- ☐
- ☐
- ☐
- ☐
- ☐
- ☐
- ☐

Pre-planned kindness:

Tic toc! Appointments

- ⊘
- ⊘
- ⊘

Something great about me

3 Gratitudes

Random Notes

Today's highlights... Best thing that happened... I did good...
Something I learned... I'm going to dream about... The funniest...

Journal

_____

_____

_____

_____

Start this day!

Today is: _____

Goals & To Do's

☐

☐

☐

☐

☐

☐

☐

☐

☐

☐

Pre-planned kindness:

Tic toc! Appointments

🕐

🕐

🕐

Something great about me

3 Gratitudes

Random Notes

Today's highlights... Best thing that happened... I did good...
Something I learned... I'm going to dream about... The funniest...

Journal

_____

_____

_____

_____

Start this day!

Today is: _____

Goals & To Do's

☐

☐

☐

☐

☐

☐

☐

☐

☐

☐

Pre-planned kindness:

Tic toc! Appointments

🕐

🕐

🕐

Something great about me

3 Gratitudes

Random Notes

Today's highlights... Best thing that happened... I did good...
Something I learned... I'm going to dream about... The funniest...

Journal

_____

_____

_____

_____

Start this day!

Today is: _____

Goals & To Do's

- [ ]
- [ ]
- [ ]
- [ ]
- [ ]
- [ ]
- [ ]
- [ ]
- [ ]
- [ ]

Pre-planned kindness:

Tic toc! Appointments

🕐
🕐
🕐

Something great about me

3 Gratitudes

Random Notes

Today's highlights... Best thing that happened... I did good...
Something I learned... I'm going to dream about... The funniest...

Journal

_____
_____
_____
_____

Start this day!

Today is: _____

Goals & To Do's

- ☐
- ☐
- ☐
- ☐
- ☐
- ☐
- ☐
- ☐
- ☐
- ☐

Pre-planned kindness:

Tic toc! Appointments

- 🕐
- 🕐
- 🕐

Something great about me

3 Gratitudes

Random Notes

Today's highlights... Best thing that happened... I did good...
Something I learned... I'm going to dream about... The funniest...

Journal

_____
_____
_____
_____

Start this day!

Today is: _____

Goals & To Do's

☐

☐

☐

☐

☐

☐

☐

☐

☐

☐

Pre-planned kindness:

Tic toc! Appointments

🕐

🕐

🕐

Something great about me

3 Gratitudes

Random Notes

Today's highlights... Best thing that happened... I did good...
Something I learned... I'm going to dream about... The funniest...

Journal

_____

_____

_____

_____

Start this day!

Today is: _____

Goals & To Do's

- ☐
- ☐
- ☐
- ☐
- ☐
- ☐
- ☐
- ☐
- ☐
- ☐

Pre-planned kindness:

Tic toc! Appointments

🕐
🕐
🕐

Something great about me

3 Gratitudes

Random Notes

Today's highlights... Best thing that happened... I did good...
Something I learned... I'm going to dream about... The funniest...

Journal

_____

_____

_____

_____

Start this day!

Today is: _____

Goals & To Do's

- ☐
- ☐
- ☐
- ☐
- ☐
- ☐
- ☐
- ☐
- ☐
- ☐

Pre-planned kindness:

Tic toc! Appointments

🕐
🕐
🕐

Something great about me

3 Gratitudes

Random Notes

Today's highlights... Best thing that happened... I did good...
Something I learned... I'm going to dream about... The funniest...

Journal

_____
_____
_____
_____

Start this day!

Today is: _____

Goals & To Do's

- [ ]
- [ ]
- [ ]
- [ ]
- [ ]
- [ ]
- [ ]
- [ ]
- [ ]
- [ ]

Pre-planned kindness:

Tic toc! Appointments

🕐
🕐
🕐

Something great about me

3 Gratitudes

Random Notes

Today's highlights... Best thing that happened... I did good...
Something I learned... I'm going to dream about... The funniest...

Journal

_____
_____
_____
_____

Start this day!

Today is: _____

Goals & To Do's

☐

☐

☐

☐

☐

☐

☐

☐

☐

☐

Pre-planned kindness:

Tic toc! Appointments

🕐

🕐

🕐

Something great about me

3 Gratitudes

Random Notes

Today's highlights... Best thing that happened... I did good...
Something I learned... I'm going to dream about... The funniest...

Journal

_____

_____

_____

_____

Start this day!

Today is: _____

Goals & To Do's

- ☐
- ☐
- ☐
- ☐
- ☐
- ☐
- ☐
- ☐
- ☐
- ☐

Pre-planned kindness:

Tic toc! Appointments

🕐
🕐
🕐

Something great about me

3 Gratitudes

Random Notes

Today's highlights... Best thing that happened... I did good...
Something I learned... I'm going to dream about... The funniest...

Journal

_____

_____

_____

_____

Start this day!

Today is: _____

Goals & To Do's

- ☐
- ☐
- ☐
- ☐
- ☐
- ☐
- ☐
- ☐
- ☐
- ☐

Pre-planned kindness:

Tic toc! Appointments

- 🕐
- 🕐
- 🕐

Something great about me

3 Gratitudes

Random Notes

Today's highlights... Best thing that happened... I did good...
Something I learned... I'm going to dream about... The funniest...

Journal

_____

_____

_____

_____

Start this day!

Today is: _____

Goals & To Do's

- ☐
- ☐
- ☐
- ☐
- ☐
- ☐
- ☐
- ☐
- ☐
- ☐

Pre-planned kindness:

Tic toc! Appointments

- 🕐
- 🕐
- 🕐

Something great about me

3 Gratitudes

Random Notes

Today's highlights... Best thing that happened... I did good...
Something I learned... I'm going to dream about... The funniest...

Journal

_____

_____

_____

_____

Start this day!

Today is: _____

Goals & To Do's

- ☐
- ☐
- ☐
- ☐
- ☐
- ☐
- ☐
- ☐
- ☐
- ☐

Pre-planned kindness:

Tic toc! Appointments

- ⊘
- ⊘
- ⊘

Something great about me

3 Gratitudes

Random Notes

Today's highlights... Best thing that happened... I did good...
Something I learned... I'm going to dream about... The funniest...

Journal

_____
_____
_____
_____

Start this day!

Today is: _____

Goals & To Do's

☐

☐

☐

☐

☐

☐

☐

☐

☐

☐

Pre-planned kindness:

Tic toc! Appointments

🕐

🕐

🕐

Something great about me

3 Gratitudes

Random Notes

Today's highlights... Best thing that happened... I did good...
Something I learned... I'm going to dream about... The funniest...

Journal

_____

_____

_____

_____

Start this day!

Today is: _____

Goals & To Do's

- ☐
- ☐
- ☐
- ☐
- ☐
- ☐
- ☐
- ☐
- ☐
- ☐

Pre-planned kindness:

Tic toc! Appointments

🕐
🕐
🕐

Something great about me

3 Gratitudes

Random Notes

Today's highlights... Best thing that happened... I did good...
Something I learned... I'm going to dream about... The funniest...

Journal

_____

_____

_____

_____

Start this day!

Today is: _____

Goals & To Do's

- ☐
- ☐
- ☐
- ☐
- ☐
- ☐
- ☐
- ☐
- ☐
- ☐

Pre-planned kindness:

Tic toc! Appointments

- 🕐
- 🕐
- 🕐

Something great about me

3 Gratitudes

Random Notes

Today's highlights... Best thing that happened... I did good...
Something I learned... I'm going to dream about... The funniest...

Journal

_____

_____

_____

_____

Start this day!

Today is: _____

Goals & To Do's

☐
☐
☐
☐
☐
☐
☐
☐
☐
☐

Pre-planned kindness:

Tic toc! Appointments

🕐
🕐
🕐

Something great about me

3 Gratitudes

Random Notes

Today's highlights... Best thing that happened... I did good...
Something I learned... I'm going to dream about... The funniest...

Journal

_____
_____
_____
_____

Start this day!

Today is: _____

Goals & To Do's

- ☐
- ☐
- ☐
- ☐
- ☐
- ☐
- ☐
- ☐
- ☐
- ☐

Pre-planned kindness:

Tic toc! Appointments

- ⊘
- ⊘
- ⊘

Something great about me

3 Gratitudes

Random Notes

Today's highlights... Best thing that happened... I did good...
Something I learned... I'm going to dream about... The funniest...

Journal

_____

_____

_____

_____

Start this day!

Today is: _____

Goals & To Do's

- ☐
- ☐
- ☐
- ☐
- ☐
- ☐
- ☐
- ☐
- ☐
- ☐

Pre-planned kindness:

Tic toc! Appointments

🕐
🕐
🕐

Something great about me

3 Gratitudes

Random Notes

Today's highlights... Best thing that happened... I did good...
Something I learned... I'm going to dream about... The funniest...

Journal

_____
_____
_____
_____

Start this day!

Today is: _____

Goals & To Do's

☐

☐

☐

☐

☐

☐

☐

☐

☐

☐

Pre-planned kindness:

Tic toc! Appointments

🕐

🕐

🕐

Something great about me

3 Gratitudes

Random Notes

Today's highlights... Best thing that happened... I did good...
Something I learned... I'm going to dream about... The funniest...

Journal

_____

_____

_____

_____

Start this day!

Today is: _____

Goals & To Do's

☐

☐

☐

☐

☐

☐

☐

☐

☐

☐

Pre-planned kindness:

Tic toc! Appointments

⊘

⊘

⊘

Something great about me

3 Gratitudes

Random Notes

Today's highlights... Best thing that happened... I did good...
Something I learned... I'm going to dream about... The funniest...

Journal

_____

_____

_____

_____

Start this day!

Today is: _____

Goals & To Do's

- ☐
- ☐
- ☐
- ☐
- ☐
- ☐
- ☐
- ☐
- ☐
- ☐

Pre-planned kindness:

Tic toc! Appointments

- ⏱
- ⏱
- ⏱

Something great about me

3 Gratitudes

Random Notes

Today's highlights... Best thing that happened... I did good...
Something I learned... I'm going to dream about... The funniest...

Journal

_____
_____
_____
_____

Start this day!

Today is: _____

Goals & To Do's

- [ ]
- [ ]
- [ ]
- [ ]
- [ ]
- [ ]
- [ ]
- [ ]
- [ ]
- [ ]

Pre-planned kindness:

Tic toc! Appointments

- 🕐
- 🕐
- 🕐

Something great about me

3 Gratitudes

Random Notes

Today's highlights... Best thing that happened... I did good...
Something I learned... I'm going to dream about... The funniest...

Journal

_____
_____
_____
_____

Start this day!

Today is: _____

Goals & To Do's

☐

☐

☐

☐

☐

☐

☐

☐

☐

☐

Pre-planned kindness:

Tic toc! Appointments
🕐
🕐
🕐

Something great about me

3 Gratitudes

Random Notes

Today's highlights... Best thing that happened... I did good...
Something I learned... I'm going to dream about... The funniest...

Journal

_____

_____

_____

_____

Start this day!

Today is: _____

Goals & To Do's

- ☐
- ☐
- ☐
- ☐
- ☐
- ☐
- ☐
- ☐
- ☐
- ☐

Pre-planned kindness:

Tic toc! Appointments

🕐
🕐
🕐

Something great about me

3 Gratitudes

Random Notes

Today's highlights... Best thing that happened... I did good...
Something I learned... I'm going to dream about... The funniest...

Journal

_____
_____
_____
_____

Start this day!

Today is: _____

Goals & To Do's

- [ ]
- [ ]
- [ ]
- [ ]
- [ ]
- [ ]
- [ ]
- [ ]
- [ ]
- [ ]

Pre-planned kindness:

Tic toc! Appointments

- ⏱
- ⏱
- ⏱

Something great about me

3 Gratitudes

Random Notes

Today's highlights... Best thing that happened... I did good...
Something I learned... I'm going to dream about... The funniest...

Journal

_____
_____
_____
_____

Start this day!

Today is: _____

Goals & To Do's

☐

☐

☐

☐

☐

☐

☐

☐

☐

☐

Pre-planned kindness:

Tic toc! Appointments

🕐
🕐
🕐

Something great about me

3 Gratitudes

Random Notes

Today's highlights... Best thing that happened... I did good...
Something I learned... I'm going to dream about... The funniest...

Journal

_____

_____

_____

_____

Start this day!

Today is: _____

Goals & To Do's

- ☐
- ☐
- ☐
- ☐
- ☐
- ☐
- ☐
- ☐
- ☐
- ☐

Pre-planned kindness:

Tic toc! Appointments

- 🕐
- 🕐
- 🕐

Something great about me

3 Gratitudes

Random Notes

Today's highlights... Best thing that happened... I did good...
Something I learned... I'm going to dream about... The funniest...

Journal

_____

_____

_____

_____

Start this day!

Today is: _____

Goals & To Do's

- [ ]
- [ ]
- [ ]
- [ ]
- [ ]
- [ ]
- [ ]
- [ ]
- [ ]
- [ ]

Pre-planned kindness:

Tic toc! Appointments
- ⏱
- ⏱
- ⏱

Something great about me

3 Gratitudes

Random Notes

Today's highlights... Best thing that happened... I did good...
Something I learned... I'm going to dream about... The funniest...

Journal

_____

_____

_____

_____

Start this day!

Today is: _____

Goals & To Do's

☐

☐

☐

☐

☐

☐

☐

☐

☐

☐

Pre-planned kindness:

Tic toc! Appointments

🕐

🕐

🕐

Something great about me

3 Gratitudes

Random Notes

Today's highlights... Best thing that happened... I did good...
Something I learned... I'm going to dream about... The funniest...

Journal

_____

_____

_____

_____

Start this day!

Today is: _____

Goals & To Do's

- ☐
- ☐
- ☐
- ☐
- ☐
- ☐
- ☐
- ☐
- ☐
- ☐

Pre-planned kindness:

Tic toc! Appointments

- ☺
- ☺
- ☺

Something great about me

3 Gratitudes

Random Notes

Today's highlights... Best thing that happened... I did good...
Something I learned... I'm going to dream about... The funniest...

Journal

_____

_____

_____

_____

Start this day!

Today is: _____

Goals & To Do's

☐
☐
☐
☐
☐
☐
☐
☐
☐
☐

Pre-planned kindness:

Tic toc! Appointments

🕐
🕐
🕐

Something great about me

3 Gratitudes

Random Notes

Today's highlights... Best thing that happened... I did good...
Something I learned... I'm going to dream about... The funniest...

Journal

_____
_____
_____
_____

Start this day!

Today is: _____

Goals & To Do's

- ☐
- ☐
- ☐
- ☐
- ☐
- ☐
- ☐
- ☐
- ☐
- ☐

Pre-planned kindness:

Tic toc! Appointments

- 🕐
- 🕐
- 🕐

Something great about me

3 Gratitudes

Random Notes

Today's highlights... Best thing that happened... I did good...
Something I learned... I'm going to dream about... The funniest...

Journal

_____
_____
_____
_____

Start this day!

Today is: _____

Goals & To Do's

- ☐
- ☐
- ☐
- ☐
- ☐
- ☐
- ☐
- ☐
- ☐
- ☐

Pre-planned kindness:

Tic toc! Appointments

🕐
🕐
🕐

Something great about me

3 Gratitudes

Random Notes

Today's highlights... Best thing that happened... I did good...
Something I learned... I'm going to dream about... The funniest...

Journal

_____

_____

_____

_____

Start this day!

Today is: _____

Goals & To Do's

- ☐
- ☐
- ☐
- ☐
- ☐
- ☐
- ☐
- ☐
- ☐
- ☐

Pre-planned kindness:

Tic toc! Appointments

- 🕐
- 🕐
- 🕐

Something great about me

3 Gratitudes

Random Notes

Today's highlights... Best thing that happened... I did good...
Something I learned... I'm going to dream about... The funniest...

Journal

_____
_____
_____
_____

Start this day!

Today is: _____

Goals & To Do's

- ☐
- ☐
- ☐
- ☐
- ☐
- ☐
- ☐
- ☐
- ☐
- ☐

Pre-planned kindness:

Tic toc! Appointments

- ⏱
- ⏱
- ⏱

Something great about me

3 Gratitudes

Random Notes

Today's highlights... Best thing that happened... I did good...
Something I learned... I'm going to dream about... The funniest...

Journal

_____
_____
_____
_____

Start this day!

Today is: _____

Goals & To Do's

- ☐
- ☐
- ☐
- ☐
- ☐
- ☐
- ☐
- ☐
- ☐
- ☐

Pre-planned kindness:

Tic toc! Appointments

🕐
🕐
🕐

Something great about me

3 Gratitudes

Random Notes

Today's highlights... Best thing that happened... I did good...
Something I learned... I'm going to dream about... The funniest...

Journal

_____

_____

_____

_____

Start this day!

Today is: _____

Goals & To Do's

- ☐
- ☐
- ☐
- ☐
- ☐
- ☐
- ☐
- ☐
- ☐
- ☐

Pre-planned kindness:

Tic toc! Appointments

- 🕐
- 🕐
- 🕐

Something great about me

3 Gratitudes

Random Notes

Today's highlights... Best thing that happened... I did good...
Something I learned... I'm going to dream about... The funniest...

Journal

_____

_____

_____

_____

Start this day!

Today is: _____

Goals & To Do's

☐
☐
☐
☐
☐
☐
☐
☐
☐
☐

Pre-planned kindness:

Tic toc! Appointments

🕐
🕐
🕐

Something great about me

3 Gratitudes

Random Notes

Today's highlights... Best thing that happened... I did good...
Something I learned... I'm going to dream about... The funniest...

Journal

_____
_____
_____
_____

Part 3 - "Help! I'm bored!"

Yes, it's bound to happen sometimes. Rainy days and the dog days of August can challenge even the most creative and active people, but never fear! Here's a list of all kinds of activities – if you still can't find something to do after reading through the list, it's time to do a chore. ☺

- Play in a creek
- Find constellations in the night sky
- Watch clouds
- Visit the planetarium for a star show
- Visit a botanical garden
- Have a yard sale
- Exercise
- Make trail mix
- Bird watching
- Catch fireflies in a jar (and then set them free)
- Build a campfire
- Yoga
- Do a 10-day detox diet
- Make your family tree
- Karaoke
- Make a music video
- Color
- Write a poem
- Host a cooking party
- Make soap
- Plan your wedding
- Ping pong
- Make dinner for the family
- Keep a journal
- Shoot pool
- Water balloon fight
- Make a summer playlist
- Write a letter
- Listen to classical music
- Draw a self portrait
- Build something with tools
- Make a collage of your dream
- Tai chi
- Go to a carnival
- Read a summer book
- Write your own memoir
- Learn basic sewing
- Bleach T-shirt designs
- Sing karaoke
- Watch an old classic movie
- Make a rap song
- Watch the sunset
- Go to a festival
- Paint your toenails

- Make a comic strip
- Learn to knit or crochet
- Paint your bedroom
- Start a scrap book
- Roller blade
- Make freezer jam
- Play Frisbee
- Try a new craft
- Take a bubble bath
- Play on a playground
- Hacky sack
- Write a play
- Play darts
- Random act of kindness
- Make a time capsule
- Practice another language
- Host a craft night
- Plan your dream vacation
- Photo scavenger hunt
- Run an errand for someone who needs help
- Go fruit picking
- Learn bird calls
- Sleepover at Grandma's
- Submit your creative work for a contest
- Watch a sunrise
- Ride scooters
- Vacuum or sweep the house – watch their surprise!
- Play with little kids
- Air hockey
- Go garage sale-ing
- Go thrift shopping with $10
- Make homemade pizza
- Rodeo
- Be a photojournalist in your neighborhood
- Write a story
- Visit or facetime your cousins
- Try a new food
- Rock climbing wall
- Spend all day riding your bike around town
- Circus
- Frisbee golf
- Clean the garage/basement/attic
- Ice cream sundae party
- Flea market
- Paint a picture
- Make fancy coffee drinks
- Sketch your dream house
- Visit a tourist attraction you've never been to in your town
- Play with sparklers on July 4th
- Wash the car
- Nature scavenger hunt
- Farmers market
- Host a board game night
- Pick a bouquet of wildflowers
- Watch old cartoons
- Squirt gun fight
- Deep clean your room – you know you need it!
- Track the moon phases

- Learn the zodiac
- Make a documentary of your summer
- Make a map of your life
- Tour a local factory
- Explore a new park
- Watch old home movies
- Set up a slip 'n slide
- Make homemade salsa
- Learn 3 new jokes
- Babysit for someone who needs a break
- Shoot hoops
- Go fishing
- Clean your room
- Host a movie night
- Plan a cook-out or BBQ
- Make jewelry
- Play cards
- Go on a road trip
- Bake a blueberry or peach pie
- Drive-in movies
- Trampoline
- Have breakfast for dinner
- Harvest all your outgrown toys and donate them
- Make waffles or pancakes
- Go bowling
- Bake cookies
- Paper airplanes
- Make a YouTube video
- Jump rope
- Do a puzzle
- Pillow fight
- Ride a train
- Go swimming
- DIY project
- Origami
- Play an instrument
- Put on a fashion show
- Pull weeds
- Learn about a country
- Play games at an arcade
- Run through the sprinkler
- Take apart an old appliance to see how it works
- Visit Mom or Dad at work
- Play two truths and a lie
- Visit a local farm
- Try a new recipe
- Go to the fair
- Visit the zoo
- Go hiking
- Roast marshmallows
- Amusement park
- Kickball
- Water park
- Have ice cream for breakfast
- Mini golf
- Go to a baseball game
- Make popsicles
- Blow bubbles
- Sidewalk chalk
- Go to the library
- Play catch
- Eat watermelon
- Plant flowers

- Play in the rain
- Bonfire
- Volleyball
- Tie-dye shirts
- Visit a museum
- Fly a kite
- Go to the movies
- Workout video
- Take silly selfies
- Bowling
- Have a sleepover
- Journal
- Geocaching
- Go to a professional sports event
- Build with legos
- Go tubing or canoeing
- Dance party
- Feed the ducks
- Rootbeer floats
- Yardwork for an elderly neighbor
- Free outdoor concert
- Learn a magic trick
- Finger-paint
- Unplug electronics for 24 hours
- Cartwheels in the grass
- Picnic
- Stand on your head
- Climb a tree
- Walk the dog
- Poetry slam
- Compose a garage band song
- Enter a contest
- Watch the full moon
- Learn to whistle
- Make fresh lemonade
- Take a nap

Part 4 – Epic Summer Highlights

Well, this is it! As The Epic Summer draws to a close, take a little time to reflect on and memorialize the highlights.

Funniest moments:

Fearless moments:

Magic moments:

Struggles:

Special Relationships:

My Summer Accomplishments

Last of all, take time to reflect on what you have achieved. Flip back through your goals and plans, and take credit for what you have done. Did you read three books, learn to water ski, start a Spanish conversation group, shower daily? Whatever it is, give yourself credit!   You don't have to have mastered anything. It's about progress, not perfection. You have the rest of your life to develop the things that interest you. Hopefully this summer you got the chance to taste and explore what does and doesn't float your boat. See you next summer!

Key Goal	Progress

Congratulations!

Take a moment to congratulate yourself. You just mastered the art of crafting a truly meaningful Summer. You could have opted for numbing your body and mind with A/C and screen time, letting the summer roll by as a quick uneventful breather between the last and next school year. But that is no way to live life.

You took the reigns and crafted a summer that was filled with meaningful installments on your dreams and goals. You expanded. You grew. And you had more fun taking charge of your destiny!

Good luck in the school year ahead. Maybe some of the things you discovered in planning your Epic Summer will be useful to you during the school year and in the rest of your life too. One thing is for certain – you deserve the best. And you can make it happen!

Certificate

Epic Summer Master